12/05   21

WELCOME TO THE U.S.A.
FLORIDA

Written by Ann Heinrichs   Illustrated by Matt Kania
Content Adviser: Dr. Robert Taylor, Professor,
Florida Institute of Technology, Melbourne, Florida

The Child's World

Published in the United States of America by The Child's World®
PO Box 326 • Chanhassen, MN 55317-0326
800-599-READ • www.childsworld.com

Photo Credits

Cover: Photodisc; frontispiece: VISIT FLORIDA.

Interior: Citrus Festival: 18; Corbis: 20 (Bettmann), 22 (Tony Roberts), 26 (Nik Wheeler); Florida Department of Environmental Protection: 14, 17; Getty Images: 15 (Hulton|Archive), 29 (Stone/Tom Raymond); Barbara Lunsford/Chiefland Activities, Inc.: 34; NASA/Kennedy Space Center: 21; VISIT FLORIDA: 6, 9, 10, 12, 25, 31, 33.

Acknowledgments

The Child's World®: Mary Berendes, Publishing Director

Editorial Directions, Inc.: E. Russell Primm, Editorial Director; Katie Marsico, Associate Editor; Judith Shiffer, Assistant Editor; Matt Messbarger, Editorial Assistant; Susan Hindman, Copy Editor; Melissa McDaniel, Proofreader; Peter Garnham, Matt Messbarger, Olivia Nellums, Chris Simms, Molly Symmonds, Katherine Trickle, Carl Stephen Wender, Fact Checkers; Tim Griffin/IndexServ, Indexer; Cian Loughlin O'Day, Photo Researcher and Editor

The Design Lab: Kathleen Petelinsek, Design and art production

Library of Congress Cataloging-in-Publication Data

Heinrichs, Ann.
  Florida / written by Ann Heinrichs ; cartography and illustrations by Matt Kania.
     p. cm. — (Welcome to the U.S.A.)
  Includes index.
  ISBN 1-59296-284-X (lib. bdg. : alk. paper)
  1. Florida—Juvenile literature. 2. Florida—Geography—Juvenile literature.
  I. Kania, Matt. II. Title. III. Series.
  F311.3.H45 2004
  975.9–dc22   2004005708

Ann Heinrichs is the author of more than 100 books for children and young adults. She has also enjoyed successful careers as a children's book editor and an advertising copywriter. Ann grew up in Fort Smith, Arkansas, and lives in Chicago, Illinois.

**About the Author
Ann Heinrichs**

Matt Kania loves maps and, as a kid, dreamed of making them. In school he studied geography and cartography, and today he makes maps for a living. Matt's favorite thing about drawing maps is learning about the places they represent. Many of the maps he has created can be found in books, magazines, videos, Web sites, and public places.

**About the
Map Illustrator
Matt Kania**

On the cover: Birds sure do have a cool view of Miami Beach!
On page one: Look! These seashells are just waiting to be part of our collection at home.

OUR FLORIDA TRIP

Florida's Nickname:
The Sunshine State

Ready for a tour of the Sunshine State? You'll find plenty to see and do there. You'll meet alligators and manatees. You'll dance in the streets and spit watermelon seeds. You'll explore space and the underwater world. Just follow the dotted line or skip around. Either way, you're in for an exciting ride. Are you all buckled up? Then we're on our way!

WELCOME TO
FLORIDA

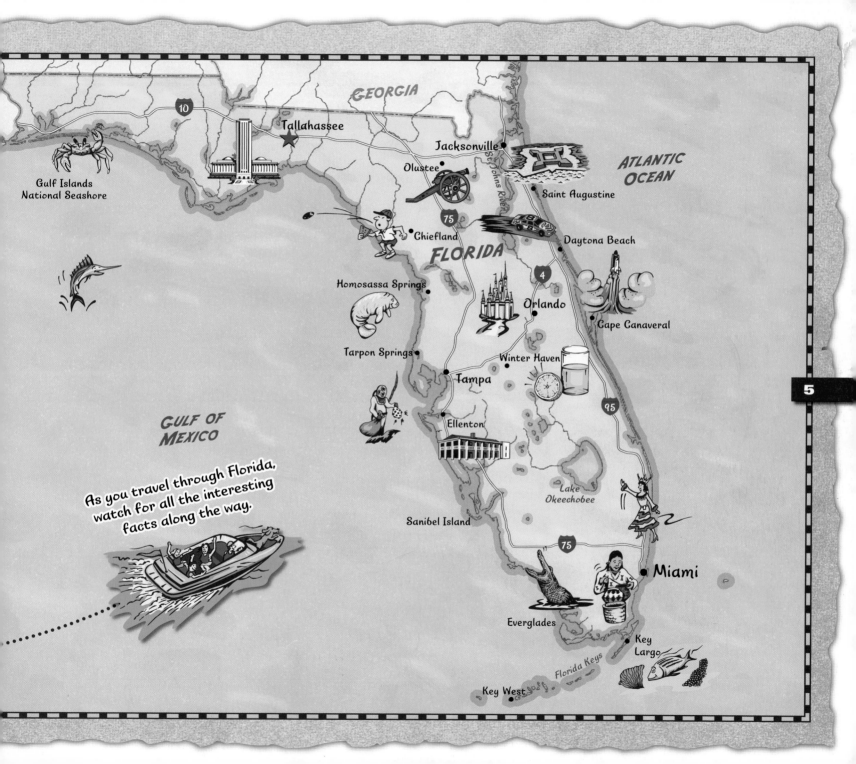

GEORGIA

Tallahassee

Jacksonville

Olustee

ATLANTIC OCEAN

Gulf Islands National Seashore

Saint Augustine

Chiefland

FLORIDA

75

Daytona Beach

4

Homosassa Springs

Orlando

Cape Canaveral

Tarpon Springs

Winter Haven

95

GULF OF MEXICO

Tampa

Ellenton

Lake Okeechobee

As you travel through Florida, watch for all the interesting facts along the way.

Sanibel Island

75

Miami

Everglades

Key Largo

Key West

Florida Keys

5

Squeaky Sand and the Panhandle

Take a step. Squeak! You're in the Florida Panhandle. And you're strolling along the beach. The sand squeaks when you walk on it!

Northwestern Florida is long and thin. It's called the Panhandle. Just imagine grabbing it like you'd grab a frying pan!

Most of Florida is a **peninsula.** The Atlantic Ocean is on the east. On the west is the Gulf of Mexico. The Everglades is a big **marshland.** It covers most of southern Florida. Islands called the Florida Keys lie off the southern coast.

Don't forget your sunscreen! Florida is famous for its beaches.

Key West has the highest average temperature in the United States.

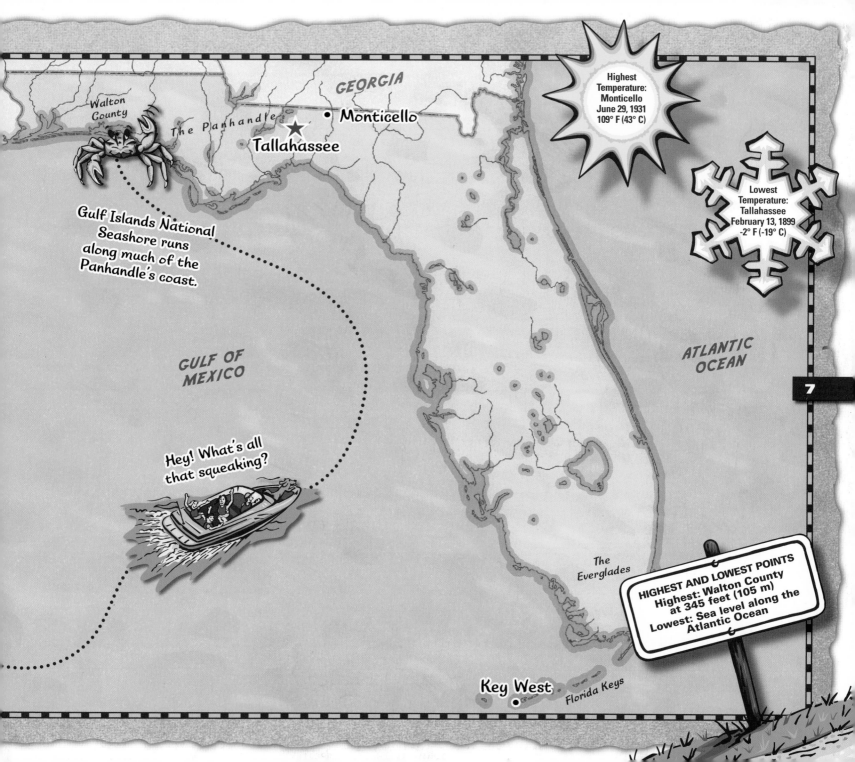

GEORGIA

Walton County

The Panhandle

• Monticello

★ Tallahassee

Gulf Islands National Seashore runs along much of the Panhandle's coast.

GULF OF MEXICO

Hey! What's all that squeaking?

ATLANTIC OCEAN

Highest Temperature: Monticello June 29, 1931 109° F (43° C)

Lowest Temperature: Tallahassee February 13, 1899 -2° F (-19° C)

The Everglades

HIGHEST AND LOWEST POINTS
Highest: Walton County at 345 feet (105 m)
Lowest: Sea level along the Atlantic Ocean

Key West • Florida Keys

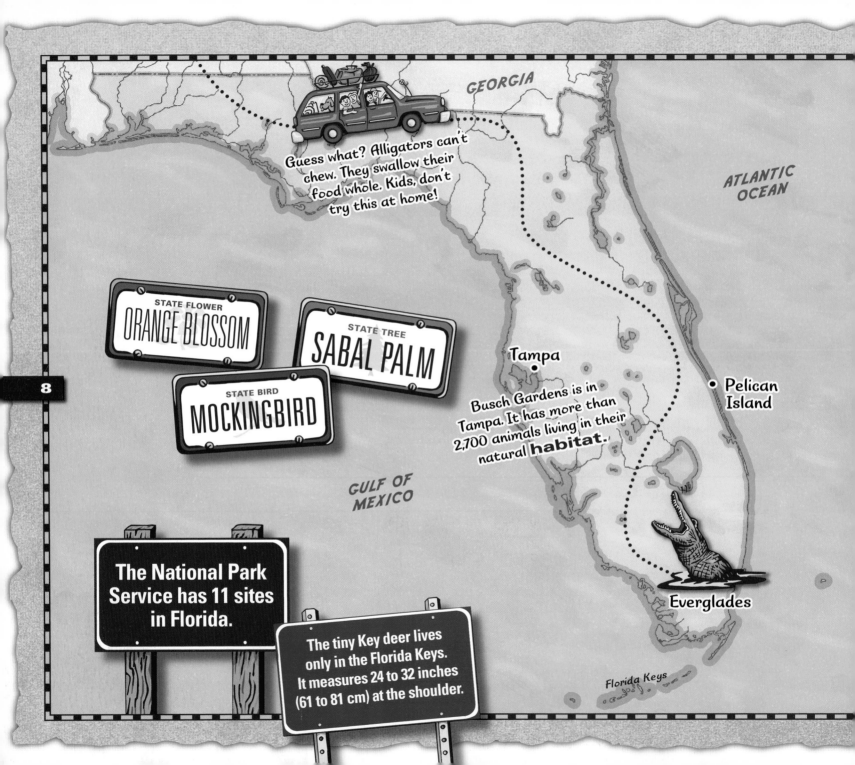

GEORGIA

ATLANTIC OCEAN

Guess what? Alligators can't chew. They swallow their food whole. Kids, don't try this at home!

STATE FLOWER
ORANGE BLOSSOM

STATE TREE
SABAL PALM

STATE BIRD
MOCKINGBIRD

Tampa

Busch Gardens is in Tampa. It has more than 2,700 animals living in their natural **habitat.**

• Pelican Island

GULF OF MEXICO

The National Park Service has 11 sites in Florida.

The tiny Key deer lives only in the Florida Keys. It measures 24 to 32 inches (61 to 81 cm) at the shoulder.

Everglades

Florida Keys

Critters in the Everglades

Watch out! Sharp-toothed gators call the Everglades home.

Snap! There goes a fish. Chomp! There goes a frog. Watch out. That alligator looks hungry. You might be next!

You're on a boat ride through the Everglades. You see turtles, snakes, and long-legged birds. Now you're face-to-face with an alligator. Keep your hands inside that boat!

The Everglades are full of animals. There are bobcats, manatees, and storks. Mangrove trees grow there, too. Spanish moss hangs down from their branches. Palm trees sway along the coast. Out in the water are fish and dolphins.

Pelican Island was the country's 1st wildlife refuge. It was set aside in 1903. Brown pelicans, herons, and egrets live there.

Want to learn about Florida's American Indians?
Head to Miccosukee Indian Village!

Spanish explorer
Hernando de Soto
reached Tampa Bay
in 1539. He met the
Timucua there.

Miccosukee Indian Village in the Everglades

A villager enters the alligator pit. He grabs the gator, and fwap! The gator's on its back and can't move!

You're visiting Miccosukee Indian Village. The alligator show is fun to watch. But don't miss the rest of the village. It shows how Florida's American Indians once lived. You'll see villagers weaving baskets and carving wood. And you'll visit their chickees, or huts.

Many American Indian groups once lived in Florida. Their lives changed forever in the 1500s. That's when Spanish explorers arrived. The Spaniards killed many American Indians in battle. They passed on diseases to them, as well.

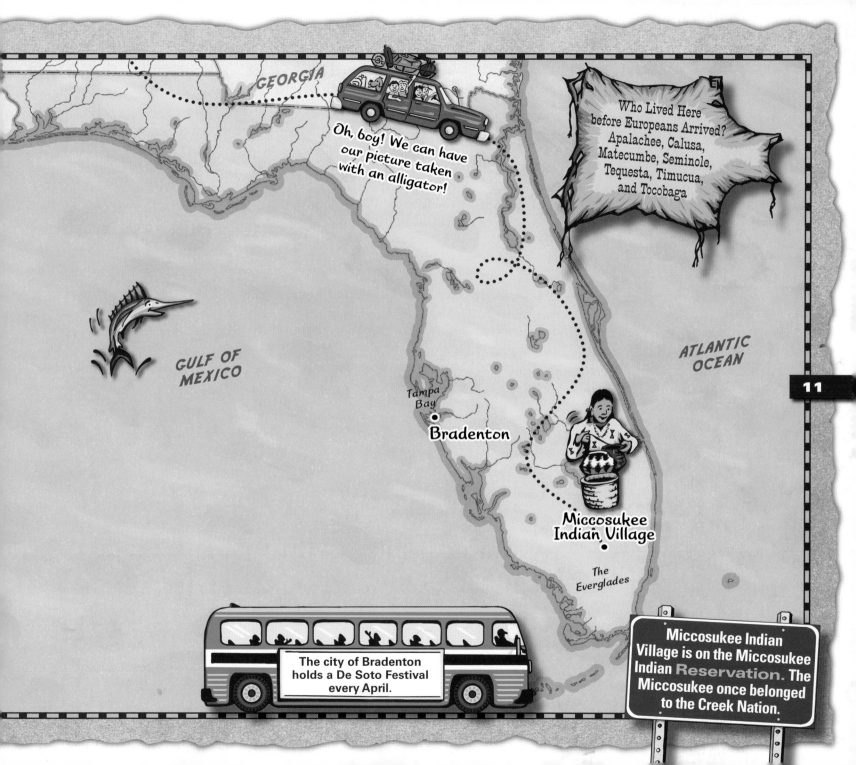

GEORGIA

Oh, boy! We can have our picture taken with an alligator!

Who Lived Here before Europeans Arrived? Apalachee, Calusa, Matecumbe, Seminole, Tequesta, Timucua, and Tocobaga

GULF OF MEXICO

ATLANTIC OCEAN

Tampa Bay

Bradenton

Miccosukee Indian Village

The Everglades

The city of Bradenton holds a De Soto Festival every April.

Miccosukee Indian Village is on the Miccosukee Indian Reservation. The Miccosukee once belonged to the Creek Nation.

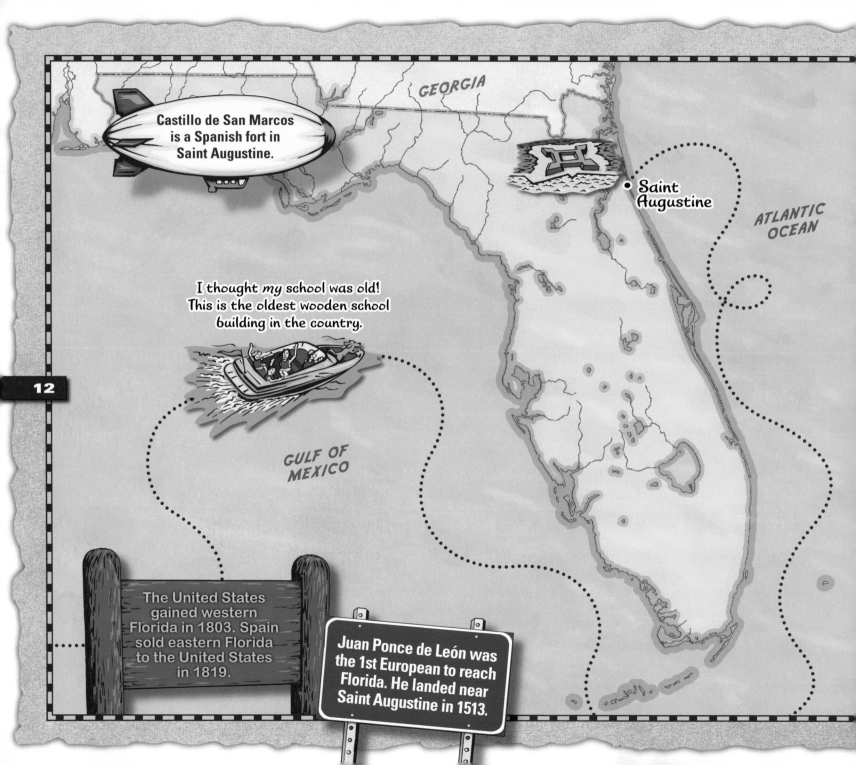

The Oldest Wooden Schoolhouse and Saint Augustine

Yikes! You'd better be good in school today. You might be sent to the basement! Well, not really. You're visiting the Oldest Wooden Schoolhouse in Saint Augustine. Your guides are a mechanical teacher and students. They tell what their school day was like. And where naughty kids were sent!

Spaniards set up Saint Augustine in 1565. It's the oldest city in the United States. Spend a day in the city's old section. You'll see the jail and a fort. You can also visit people's homes. They show you what everyday life was like. And don't worry about that schoolhouse. It's a friendly place. You even get a **diploma** when you leave!

What was school like in the 1700s? Visit Saint Augustine and find out!

How did Floridians live in the mid-1800s? Tour Gamble Plantation and see for yourself.

Robert Gamble built Gamble Plantation in 1844. He grew sugarcane there. African American slaves worked the fields.

Gamble Plantation and the Sugarcane Farms

The **mansion** at Ellenton's Gamble Plantation is a tabby house. That means it's made of tabby. Tabby is seashells mixed with sand. It looks sort of speckled, but it doesn't meow!

Spain gave up Florida in 1819. Then American settlers poured in. Some built huge farms called plantations. They grew sugarcane and other crops. Many built their homes out of tabby.

The settlers wanted the Native Americans out of the way. The Seminole people fought hard to stay. Chief Osceola had them hide in the **swamps.** Finally, most Seminoles were driven out.

GEORGIA

We've got a tabby cat. It's speckled all over. But what's a tabby house? A house full of tabby cats?

GULF OF MEXICO

ATLANTIC OCEAN

• Ellenton

The United States fought 3 wars against the Seminole people. The Seminole Wars lasted from 1817 to 1858.

Dear Osceola:
You were very brave.
You agreed to talk
about peace in 1837.
Instead, you were
thrown in jail. Then
you died.
            Sadly,
            A friend

Chief Osceola
ca. 1804–1838
The Everglades, FL

The
Everglades

Gamble Plantation holds an open house every spring. People there dress in 1800s style. They demonstrate crafts from that time.

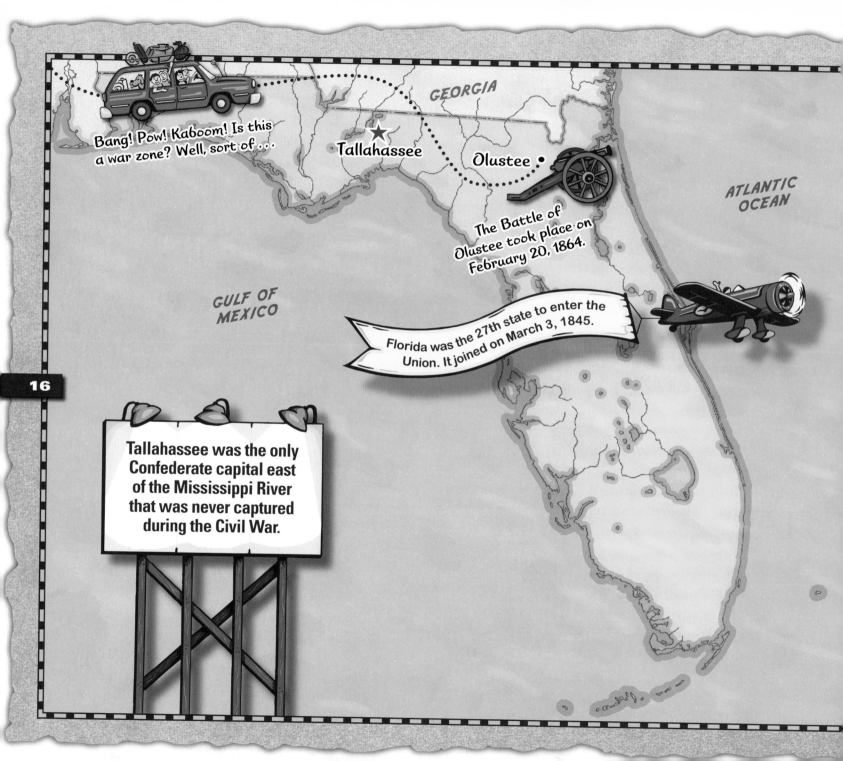

GEORGIA

Bang! Pow! Kaboom! Is this a war zone? Well, sort of ...

★ Tallahassee

Olustee •

ATLANTIC OCEAN

The Battle of Olustee took place on February 20, 1864.

GULF OF MEXICO

Florida was the 27th state to enter the Union. It joined on March 3, 1845.

Tallahassee was the only Confederate capital east of the Mississippi River that was never captured during the Civil War.

The Battle of Olustee and the Civil War

Watch out! Cannons are booming! Men on horseback are swishing swords! It's the Battle of Olustee!

People act out this battle every year. It took place during the Civil War (1861–1865). Northern and Southern states fought this war over slavery. Florida joined the South, or Confederate side.

The Battle of Olustee was Florida's biggest Civil War battle. Confederates won the battle. But the North won the war. Then all the slaves were freed.

Railroads began bringing tourists to Florida in the 1880s. Swamps were drained to create more dry land. Then many farmers started growing citrus trees.

Cannons, gunfire, and men on horseback! People act out the Battle of Olustee every February.

Florida declared itself an independent nation in January 1861. A month later, it joined other Southern states in the Confederate States of America.

Quiz time! Cross a tangerine with a grapefruit, and what do you get? A tangelo!

Whoosh! There goes the roller coaster. Smash! That's the bumper cars. Glub, glub. That's no ride. It's the Jell-O eating contest!

You're at the Florida Citrus Festival in Winter Haven. It celebrates Florida's top crops—citrus fruits. They include oranges, grapefruits, and lemons. You know. The fruits that make your face squinch up!

18

How about a nice juicy orange? Stop by the Florida Citrus Festival!

Tangerines are called zipper fruits because they peel so easily.

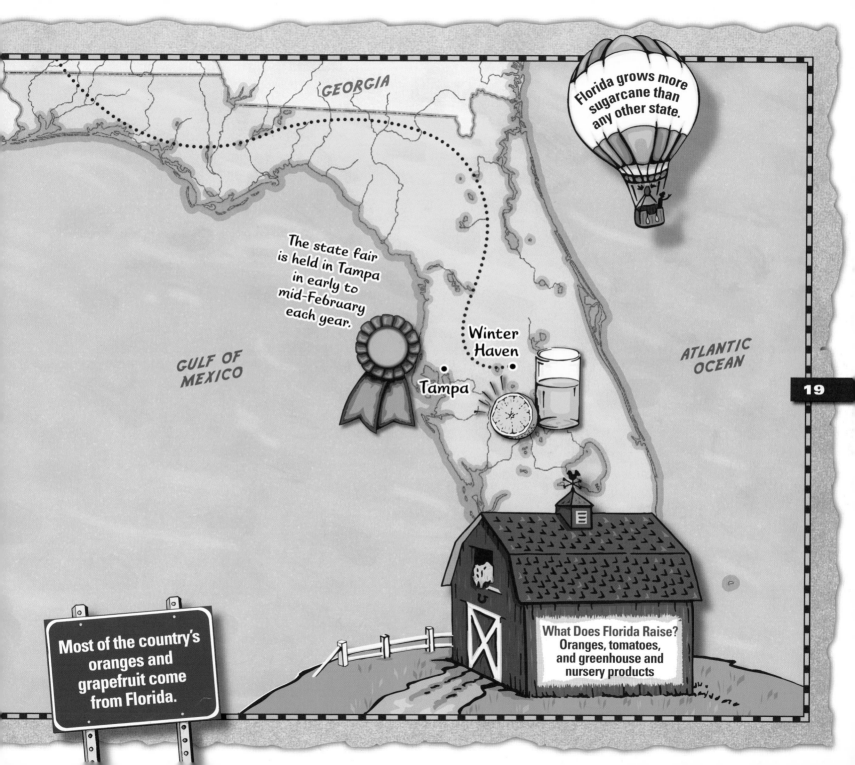

GEORGIA

Florida grows more sugarcane than any other state.

The state fair is held in Tampa in early to mid-February each year.

GULF OF MEXICO

Winter Haven

Tampa

ATLANTIC OCEAN

What Does Florida Raise? Oranges, tomatoes, and greenhouse and nursery products

Most of the country's oranges and grapefruit come from Florida.

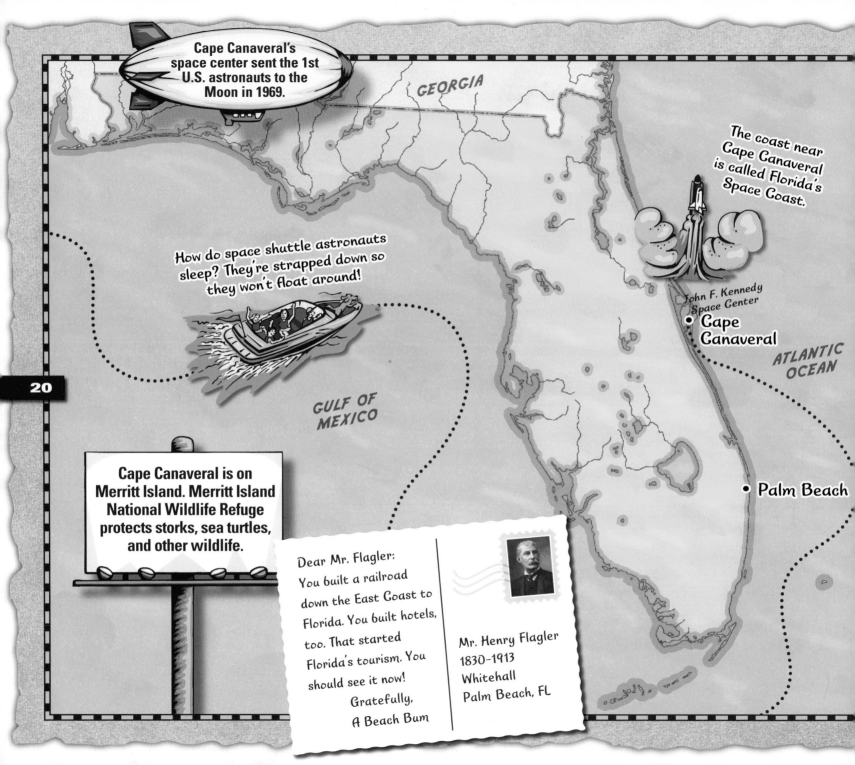

Cape Canaveral's space center sent the 1st U.S. astronauts to the Moon in 1969.

GEORGIA

The coast near Cape Canaveral is called Florida's Space Coast.

How do space shuttle astronauts sleep? They're strapped down so they won't float around!

John F. Kennedy Space Center

• Cape Canaveral

ATLANTIC OCEAN

GULF OF MEXICO

Cape Canaveral is on Merritt Island. Merritt Island National Wildlife Refuge protects storks, sea turtles, and other wildlife.

• Palm Beach

Dear Mr. Flagler:
You built a railroad down the East Coast to Florida. You built hotels, too. That started Florida's tourism. You should see it now!
Gratefully,
A Beach Bum

Mr. Henry Flagler
1830-1913
Whitehall
Palm Beach, FL

"Five, four, three, two, one. You are go for launch." Fires blaze amid clouds of smoke. The shuttle blasts off into the sky! You're at the John F. Kennedy Space Center at Cape Canaveral. And you've just watched a space shuttle launch.

Cape Canaveral opened in 1950. It became an important space center. Visitors can tour the center. If they're lucky, they'll see a launch!

Florida grew fast in the 1900s. Millions of people came as tourists. And millions moved there to live. Some came to take jobs in the state. Others came to retire in the warm climate.

Want to see a real space shuttle? Visit the John F. Kennedy Space Center.

21

Why do astronauts eat tortillas instead of bread? Because tortillas don't crumble! Bread crumbs would float around in the weightless conditions of space flight.

Okay, kids—what'll it be? Cinderella's Castle or the Tower of Terror?

E ek! We're in the Tower of Terror. We're plunging thirteen stories down! And they call this the Happiest Place on Earth? They sure do! It's Walt Disney World in Orlando. The tower is at the park's Disney-MGM Studios site.

Tourism is a big business in Florida. Millions of people visit Disney World every year. But Florida has lots of other **industries,** too. Its factories make computers, airplanes, and orange juice.

Florida's mines produce phosphate rock. It's made into **fertilizer.** Florida is a big fishing state, too. Just look at that long coastline!

Wipeout! Splash Mountain is one of Disney World's wildest rides.

About 60 million tourists visit Florida every year!

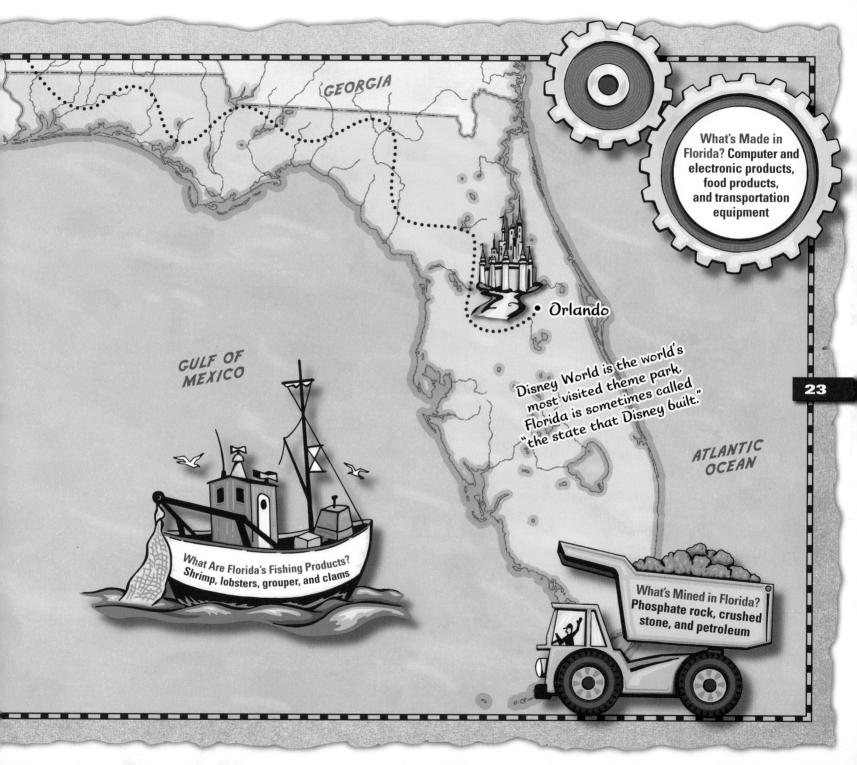

GEORGIA

GULF OF
MEXICO

ATLANTIC
OCEAN

• Orlando

What's Made in Florida? Computer and electronic products, food products, and transportation equipment

Disney World is the world's most visited theme park. Florida is sometimes called "the state that Disney built."

What Are Florida's Fishing Products? Shrimp, lobsters, grouper, and clams

What's Mined in Florida? Phosphate rock, crushed stone, and petroleum

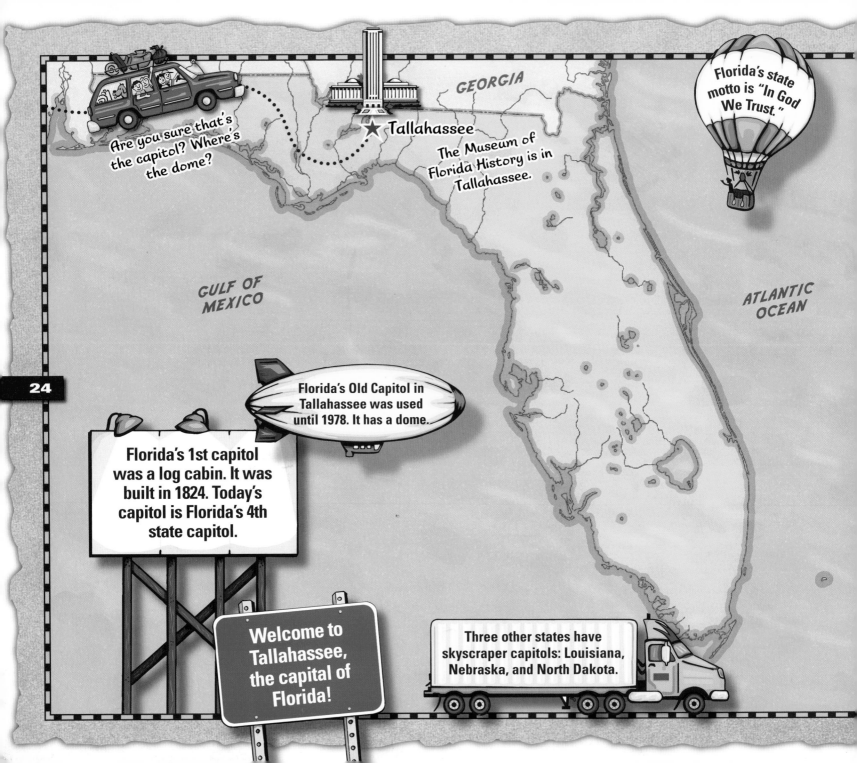

Are you sure that's the capitol? Where's the dome?

GEORGIA

★ Tallahassee

The Museum of Florida History is in Tallahassee.

Florida's state motto is "In God We Trust."

GULF OF MEXICO

ATLANTIC OCEAN

Florida's Old Capitol in Tallahassee was used until 1978. It has a dome.

Florida's 1st capitol was a log cabin. It was built in 1824. Today's capitol is Florida's 4th state capitol.

Welcome to Tallahassee, the capital of Florida!

Three other states have skyscraper capitols: Louisiana, Nebraska, and North Dakota.

The Skyscraper Capitol in Tallahassee

In most states, you can spot the state capitol. It's a few stories high. And it has a big, round **dome** on top. But Florida's capitol is a **skyscraper.** It's twenty-two stories high! And its roof is flat. You can take a tour to the top. Look around, and you'll see for miles!

Many state government offices are in the capitol. Florida has three branches of government. One branch makes laws. Its members come from all over the state. The governor heads another branch. It carries out the laws. Courts make up the third branch. They decide whether someone has broken the law.

Florida's state capitol is unusual. It's 1 of America's 4 skyscraper capitols.

Florida's capitol is 514 feet (157 m) high. That's taller than Florida's highest point of land!

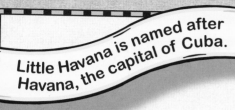

Little Havana is named after Havana, the capital of Cuba.

S narf down some **arepas.**
Dance the **merengue.**
Sneak between a stilt walker's legs.
You're at Calle Ocho!

Calle Ocho began as a Cuban festival. Now it's the biggest **Hispanic** festival in the country. It's held in Miami's Little Havana neighborhood.

Florida is home to many Cubans, Haitians, and Jamaicans. Their homelands are islands south of Florida. Many older people retire to Florida, too. Florida's population just keeps on growing. Only three states have more people.

Calle Ocho is a celebration of Cuban culture.

About 1 out of every 6 Floridians is Hispanic, or Latino. About 1 out of every 7 Floridians is African American.

26

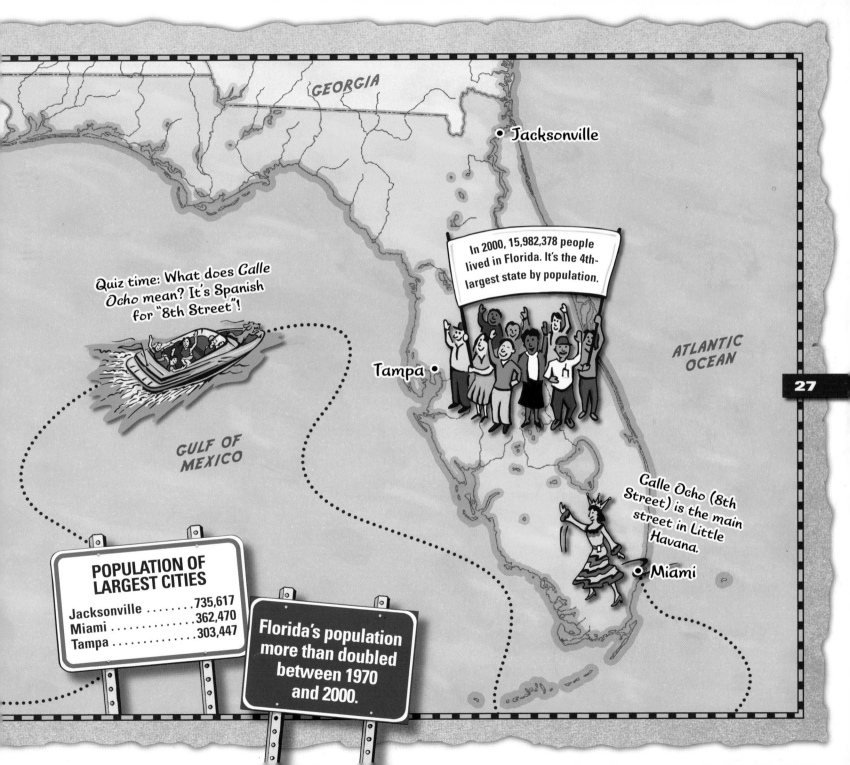

GEORGIA

• Jacksonville

Quiz time: What does *Calle Ocho* mean? It's Spanish for "8th Street"!

In 2000, 15,982,378 people lived in Florida. It's the 4th-largest state by population.

ATLANTIC OCEAN

Tampa •

GULF OF MEXICO

Calle Ocho (8th Street) is the main street in Little Havana.

• Miami

POPULATION OF LARGEST CITIES

Jacksonville 735,617
Miami 362,470
Tampa 303,447

Florida's population more than doubled between 1970 and 2000.

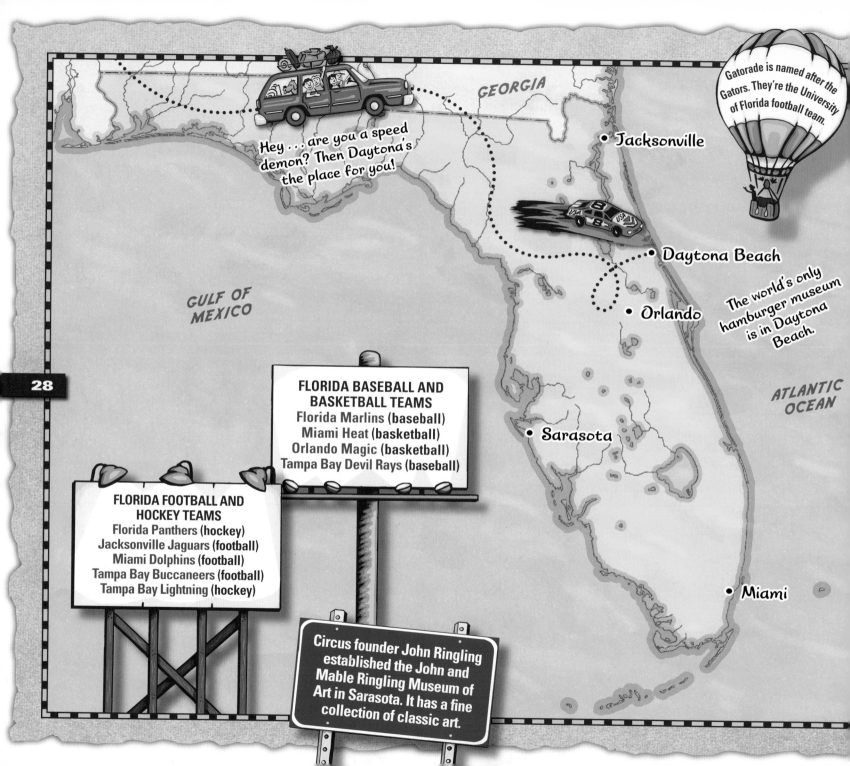

Gatorade is named after the Gators. They're the University of Florida football team.

GEORGIA

Hey . . . are you a speed demon? Then Daytona's the place for you!

Jacksonville

GULF OF MEXICO

Daytona Beach

The world's only hamburger museum is in Daytona Beach.

Orlando

ATLANTIC OCEAN

FLORIDA BASEBALL AND BASKETBALL TEAMS
Florida Marlins (baseball)
Miami Heat (basketball)
Orlando Magic (basketball)
Tampa Bay Devil Rays (baseball)

Sarasota

FLORIDA FOOTBALL AND HOCKEY TEAMS
Florida Panthers (hockey)
Jacksonville Jaguars (football)
Miami Dolphins (football)
Tampa Bay Buccaneers (football)
Tampa Bay Lightning (hockey)

Miami

Circus founder John Ringling established the John and Mable Ringling Museum of Art in Sarasota. It has a fine collection of classic art.

Daytona USA

Vroom! You're up to 200 miles (322 kilometers) an hour. Screech! You're rounding a corner four stories high. You're in the driver's seat at Daytona USA!

Daytona USA is a theme park for racing fans. It's right by the Daytona International Speedway in Daytona Beach. That's where the Daytona 500 car races are held.

Racing is just one of Florida's popular sports. Football fans enjoy the New Year's bowl games. Other people like quieter fun. They relax on the sunny beaches. They swim in the ocean. They watch wildlife or collect seashells. What would *you* do in Florida?

Do you have a need for speed? The Daytona 500 has fast racing action.

Florida's Football Bowl Games
Citrus Bowl—Orlando
Gator Bowl—Jacksonville
Orange Bowl—Miami

Manatees are nicknamed "sea cows." But they don't say moo!

John Pennekamp Coral Reef State Park

SeaWorld Orlando is the world's largest marine park. You'll see dolphin and killer whale shows there.

Animal Quiz Number One: It lives in the sea. It might be pink, orange, purple, or green. And its skeleton can sink ships. What is it? Coral! Just visit John Pennekamp Coral Reef State Park. It's near Key Largo. Take a glass-bottom boat tour. You'll see jillions of corals. Their skeletons make big underwater banks called reefs.

Animal Quiz Number Two: They're big. They're gray. Spanish sailors thought they were mermaids. What are they? They're manatees! You can watch them underwater at Homosassa Springs Wildlife Park. This park also cares for injured manatees. They often get hurt by boats.

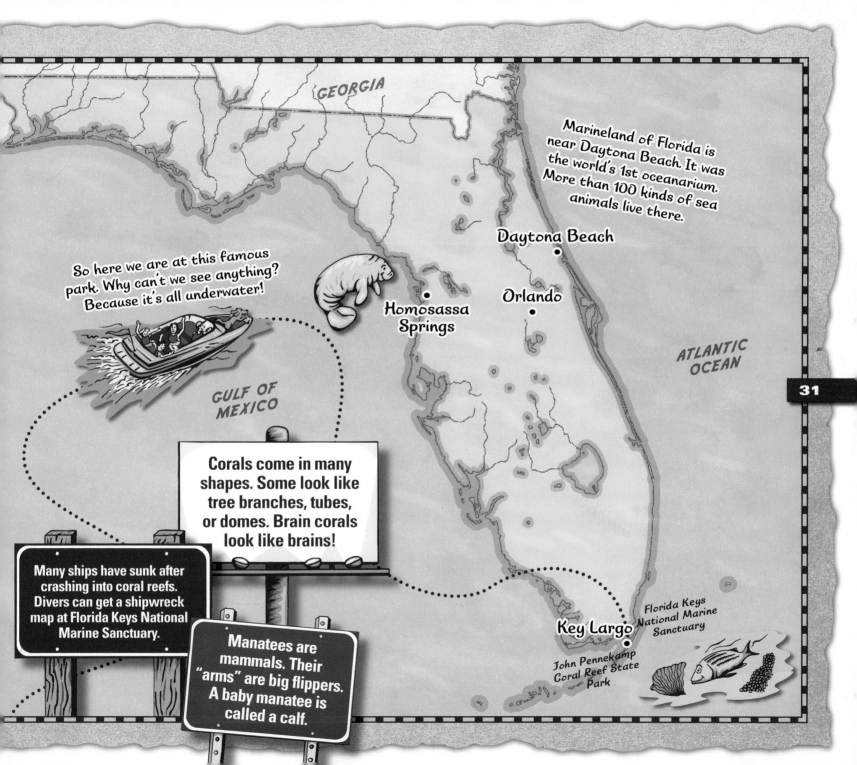

GEORGIA

Marineland of Florida is near Daytona Beach. It was the world's 1st oceanarium. More than 100 kinds of sea animals live there.

Daytona Beach

So here we are at this famous park. Why can't we see anything? Because it's all underwater!

Homosassa Springs

Orlando

ATLANTIC OCEAN

GULF OF MEXICO

Corals come in many shapes. Some look like tree branches, tubes, or domes. Brain corals look like brains!

Many ships have sunk after crashing into coral reefs. Divers can get a shipwreck map at Florida Keys National Marine Sanctuary.

Manatees are mammals. Their "arms" are big flippers. A baby manatee is called a calf.

Key Largo

Florida Keys National Marine Sanctuary

John Pennekamp Coral Reef State Park

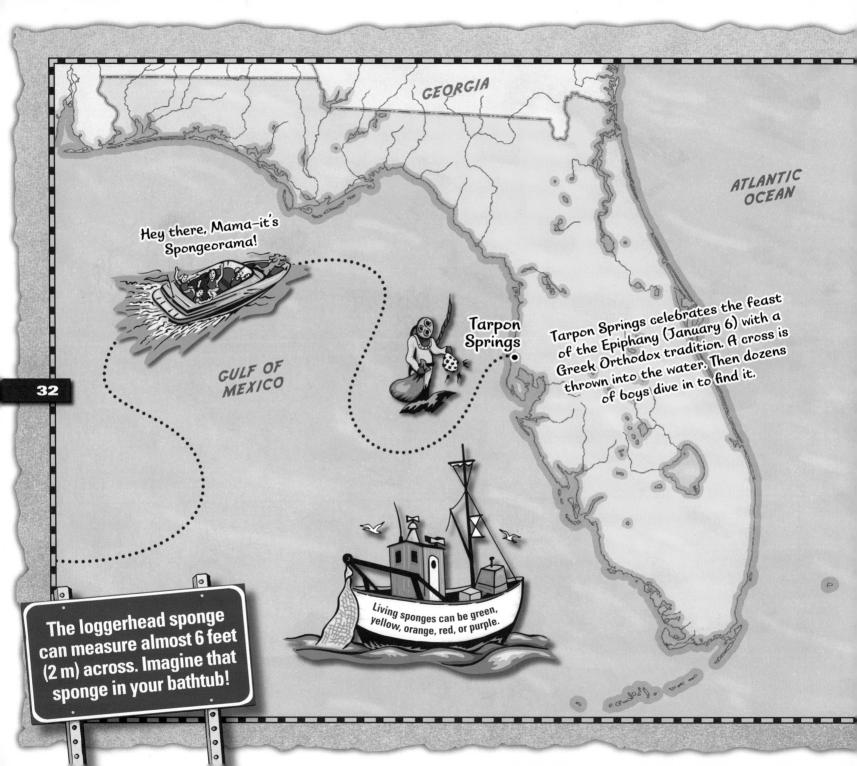

GEORGIA

ATLANTIC OCEAN

Hey there, Mama—it's Spongeorama!

GULF OF MEXICO

Tarpon Springs

Tarpon Springs celebrates the feast of the Epiphany (January 6) with a Greek Orthodox tradition. A cross is thrown into the water. Then dozens of boys dive in to find it.

Living sponges can be green, yellow, orange, red, or purple.

The loggerhead sponge can measure almost 6 feet (2 m) across. Imagine that sponge in your bathtub!

Sponges in Tarpon Springs

Animal Quiz Number Three: It lives in the sea. It's full of holes. And it has no brain. What is it? It's a sponge!

Most sponges you see today are factory-made. But natural sponges are living things. Divers harvest the sponges from the sea.

Tarpon Springs is the sponge capital of the world. Greek **immigrants** settled there in the early 1900s. They were experts at diving for sponges. A local museum tells all about sponge diving. The museum is called Spongeorama!

Want to buy a sea sponge? Just visit Tarpon Springs!

Sponges are animals with no head and no arms. They have no organs such as stomachs and hearts.

The Watermelon Festival in Chiefland

Oh, boy! Let's all spit watermelon seeds!

Thwit! Darn. That one hit a tree. Thwat! Oops. That one hit a dog. Are you any better at spitting watermelon seeds? Then come to the Chiefland Watermelon Festival!

Watermelons are an important Florida crop. Several Florida towns have watermelon festivals. They include Chiefland, Monticello, Chipley, and Newberry. Their seed-spitting contests are big hits. So are the melon-eating contests.

So how far can *you* spit a seed? Warning: Don't try it in the house!

Hungry? Dig into a watermelon at Chiefland!

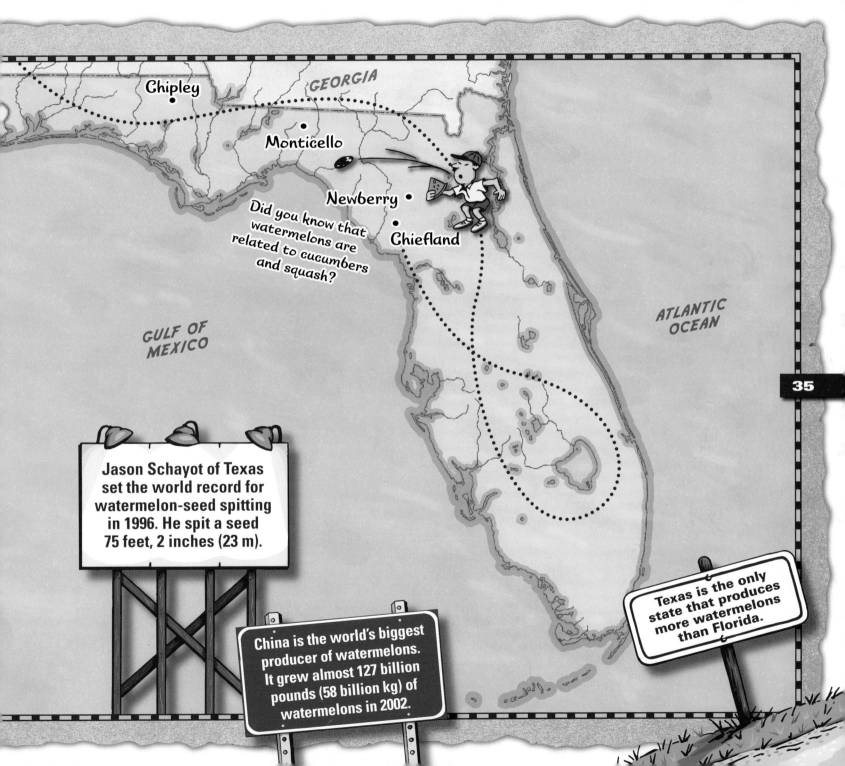

Chipley

GEORGIA

Monticello

Newberry

Did you know that watermelons are related to cucumbers and squash?

Chiefland

GULF OF MEXICO

ATLANTIC OCEAN

Jason Schayot of Texas set the world record for watermelon-seed spitting in 1996. He spit a seed 75 feet, 2 inches (23 m).

Texas is the only state that produces more watermelons than Florida.

China is the world's biggest producer of watermelons. It grew almost 127 billion pounds (58 billion kg) of watermelons in 2002.

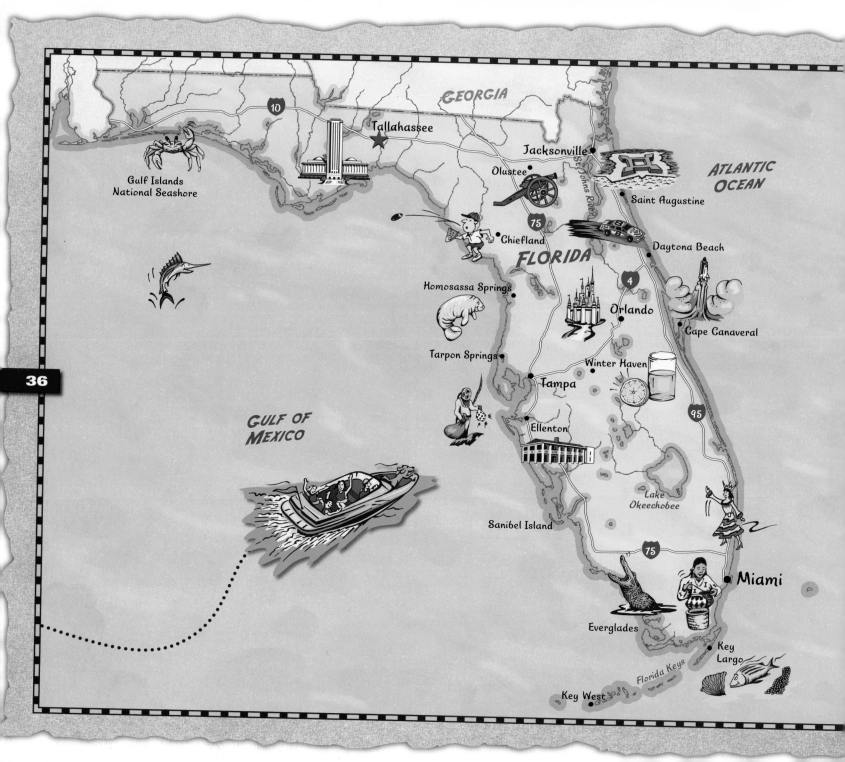

GEORGIA

10

Tallahassee

Jacksonville

Olustee

ATLANTIC OCEAN

Gulf Islands National Seashore

Saint Augustine

St. Johns River

75

Chiefland

FLORIDA

Daytona Beach

4

Homosassa Springs

Orlando

Cape Canaveral

Tarpon Springs

Winter Haven

95

Tampa

GULF OF MEXICO

Ellenton

Lake Okeechobee

Sanibel Island

75

Miami

Everglades

Key Largo

Florida Keys

Key West

OUR TRIP

We visited many amazing places on our trip! We also met a lot of interesting people along the way. Look at the map on the left. Use your finger to trace all the places we have been.

What do alligators do if they can't chew? See page 8 for the answer.

Who was the 1st European to reach Florida? Page 12 has the answer.

When did the Battle of Olustee take place? See page 16 for the answer.

Why are tangerines called zipper fruits? Look on page 18 for the answer.

How many tourists visit Florida every year? Page 22 has the answer.

What is the main street in Little Havana? Turn to page 27 for the answer.

What is a baby manatee called? Look on page 31 and find out!

Who set the world record for watermelon-seed spitting? Turn to page 35 for the answer.

That was a great trip! We have traveled all over Florida!

There are a few places that we didn't have time for, though. Next time, we plan to collect seashells on Sanibel Island. Sanibel is known as one of the best shelling spots in the world. Visitors can find more than 400 different types of shells there!

More Places to Visit in Florida

WORDS TO KNOW

arepas (uh-REE-pas) grilled cornmeal cakes

diploma (duh-PLOH-muh) a paper that says someone has completed a grade or a school

dome (DOHM) a rounded form on top of a building

fertilizer (FUR-tuh-lize-ur) plant food

habitat (HAB-uh-tat) the place and natural conditions in which a plant or an animal lives

Hispanic (hiss-PAN-ik) having roots in Spanish-speaking lands

immigrants (IM-uh-gruhnts) people who leave their home country for a new country

industries (IN-duh-streez) types of business

mansion (MAN-shuhn) a very large, fancy house

marshland (MARSH-land) a region of soft, wet land with grasses growing in it

merengue (muh-RAYN-gay) a dance from Haiti and the Dominican Republic

peninsula (puh-NIN-suh-luh) an area of land that is mostly surrounded by water

reservation (rez-ur-VAY-shuhn) land set aside for use by a group such as American Indians

skyscraper (SKYE-skray-pur) a very tall, narrow building

swamps (SWAHMPS) wetlands

Florida covers 53,927 square miles (139,670 sq km). It's the 26th-largest state in size.

STATE SYMBOLS

State animal: Florida panther

State beverage: Orange juice

State bird: Mockingbird

State butterfly: Zebra longwing

State flower: Orange blossom

State freshwater fish: Largemouth bass

State gem: Moonstone

State marine mammal: Manatee

State reptile: Alligator

State saltwater fish: Sailfish

State saltwater mammal: Dolphin

State shell: Horse conch

State stone: Agatized coral

State tree: Sabal palm

State wildflower: Coreopsis

State flag

State seal

STATE SONG

"The Swanee River"
(also called "Old Folks at Home")

Words and music by Stephen C. Foster

'Way down upon the
  Swanee River,
Far, far away,
There's where my heart is
  turning ever,
There's where the old folks stay.
All up and down the whole
  creation
Sadly I roam,
Still longing for the old
  plantation,
And for the old folks at home.

Chorus:
All the world is sad and dreary,
Everywhere I roam;
Oh, brothers, how my heart
  grows weary,
Far from the old folks at home!

All 'round the little farm
  I wandered
When I was young,
Then many happy days
  I squandered,
Many the songs I sung.
When I was playing with
  my brother
Happy was I;
Oh, take me to my kind
  old mother!
There let me live and die.

One little hut among the
  bushes,
One that I love,
Still sadly to my memory rushes,
No matter where I rove.
When will I see the bees
  a-humming
All 'round the comb?
When shall I hear the banjo
  strumming,
Down in my good old home?

FAMOUS PEOPLE

Arnaz, Desi (1917–1986), musician and television star

Bethune, Mary McLeod (1875–1955), educator and reformer

Carlton, Steve (1944–), baseball player

Edison, Thomas Alva (1847–1931), inventor

Estefan, Gloria (1957–), singer

Hemingway, Ernest (1899–1961), author

Homer, Winslow (1836–1910), artist

Hurston, Zora Neale (1891–1960), author

Johnson, James Weldon (1871–1938), author, civil rights leader

McQueen, Butterfly (1911–1995), actor

Morrison, Jim (1943–1971), rock star

Osceola (ca. 1800–1838), Seminole Indian chief

Ponce de Léon, Juan (1460–1521), explorer

Poitier, Sidney (1927–), actor

Rawlings, Marjorie Kinnan (1896–1953), author

Reno, Janet (1938–), attorney general

Ringling, John (1866–1936), circus owner

Robinson, David (1965–), basketball player

Stowe, Harriet Beecher (1811–1896), author

Versace, Gianni (1946–1997), fashion designer

TO FIND OUT MORE

At the Library

Crane, Carol, and Michael Glenn Monroe (illustrator). *S Is for Sunshine: A Florida Alphabet.* Chelsea, Mich.: Sleeping Bear Press, 2000.

George, Jean Craighead. *The Missing `Gator of Gumbo Limbo: An Ecological Mystery.* New York: HarperCollins, 1992.

Greenburg, Dan, and Jack E. Davis (illustrator). *How to Speak Dolphin in Three Easy Lessons.* New York: Grosset & Dunlap, 1997.

Pancella, Peggy. *Hernando de Soto.* Chicago: Heinemann Library, 2004.

Todd, Anne M. *Osceola.* Chicago: Heinemann Library, 2004.

On the Web

Visit our home page for lots of links about Florida:
http://www.childsworld.com/links

Note to Parents, Teachers, and Librarians: We routinely verify our Web links to make sure they are safe, active sites—so encourage your readers to check them out!

Places to Visit or Contact

Historical Museum of Southern Florida
101 West Flagler Street
Miami, FL 33130
305/375-1492
For more information about the history of Florida

Visit Florida
661 East Jefferson Street
Suite 300
Tallahassee, FL 32301
888/735-2872
For more information about traveling in Florida

INDEX

Bye, Sunshine State.
We had a great time.
We'll come back soon!